2
1/17
1/24

LIFE IN A
Coral Reef

by Kari Schuetz

BELLWETHER MEDIA • MINNEAPOLIS, MN

BLASTOFF!
3
READERS

Note to Librarians, Teachers, and Parents:

Blastoff! Readers are carefully developed by literacy experts and combine standards-based content with developmentally appropriate text.

Level 1 provides the most support through repetition of high-frequency words, light text, predictable sentence patterns, and strong visual support.

Level 2 offers early readers a bit more challenge through varied simple sentences, increased text load, and less repetition of high-frequency words.

Level 3 advances early-fluent readers toward fluency through increased text and concept load, less reliance on visuals, longer sentences, and more literary language.

Level 4 builds reading stamina by providing more text per page, increased use of punctuation, greater variation in sentence patterns, and increasingly challenging vocabulary.

Level 5 encourages children to move from "learning to read" to "reading to learn" by providing even more text, varied writing styles, and less familiar topics.

Whichever book is right for your reader, Blastoff! Readers are the perfect books to build confidence and encourage a love of reading that will last a lifetime!

This edition first published in 2016 by Bellwether Media, Inc.

No part of this publication may be reproduced in whole or in part without written permission of the publisher. For information regarding permission, write to Bellwether Media, Inc., Attention: Permissions Department, 5357 Penn Avenue South, Minneapolis, MN 55419.

Library of Congress Cataloging-in-Publication Data

Names: Schuetz, Kari.
Title: Life in a Coral Reef / by Kari Schuetz.
Description: Minneapolis, MN : Bellwether Media, Inc., 2016. | Series: Blastoff! Readers: Biomes Alive! | Includes bibliographical references and index.
Identifiers: LCCN 2015033093 | ISBN 9781626173156 (hardcover : alk. paper)
Subjects: LCSH: Coral reef ecology–Juvenile literature. | Coral reefs and islands–Juvenile literature.
Classification: LCC QH541.5.C7 S42 2016 | DDC 577.7/89–dc23
LC record available at http://lccn.loc.gov/2015033093

Printed in the United States of America, North Mankato, MN.

Table of Contents

The Coral Reef Biome   4

The Climate   8

The Plants   12

The Animals   16

The Great Barrier Reef   20

Glossary   22

To Learn More   23

Index   24

The Coral Reef Biome

Coral reefs are among the world's most colorful **biomes**! Many beautiful plants and animals live there.

Tube-shaped animals called **coral polyps** build up reefs over time. They grow hard **skeletons** and attach to those of dead corals.

coral polyps

Most coral reefs lie in the warm **tropics**. There are three main types of tropical reefs.

tropical coral reefs =

equator

N
W   E
S

Fringing reefs stretch along shores. **Barrier** reefs are farther out. Ring-shaped **atolls** rise from sunken islands.

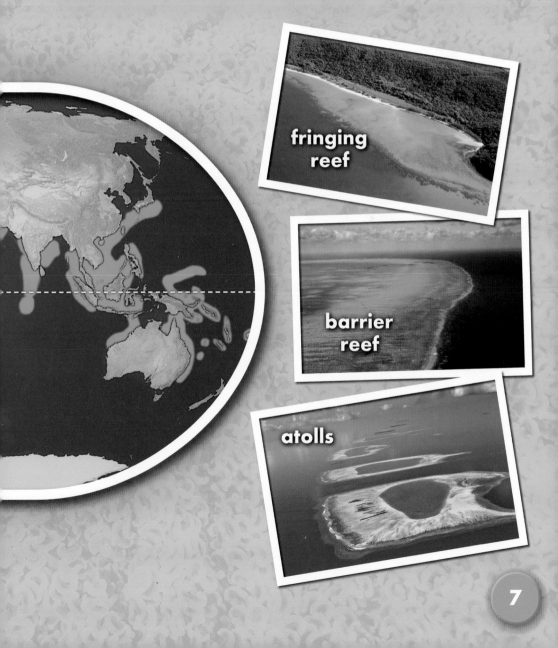

fringing reef

barrier reef

atolls

The Climate

Red Sea coral reef

Tropical coral reefs have a warm **climate**. The sun shines through the clear, shallow salt water.

Water temperatures usually stay between 65 and 85 degrees Fahrenheit (18 and 29 degrees Celsius).

Kimbe Bay coral reef

Too much wind and rain can move rocks and mud into shallow reefs. The clear water becomes cloudy.

Ningaloo Reef

Then less sunlight reaches
reef plants. This can affect the
whole coral reef **food chain**.

The Plants

algae in
coral polyps

Tiny **algae** grow all over warm coral reefs. The algae live inside of coral polyps. The animals and algae trade gases they need to live.

Larger algae called seaweeds color coral reefs. Red seaweeds grow in deeper water than green ones. Their color helps them capture more sunlight.

red seaweed

Meadows of sea grass often form around coral reefs. They provide animals with food to eat and nurseries for babies.

green sea turtle

sea grass

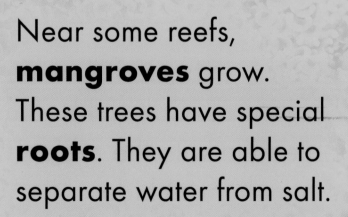
mangroves

Near some reefs,
mangroves grow.
These trees have special
roots. They are able to
separate water from salt.

The Animals

pharaoh
cuttlefish

Coral reefs are full of strange
creatures. Colorful bodies let many
blend in with the reefs. This helps
them hunt or hide.

Flat animals move through tight spaces. Pointed ones protect themselves or poke their food. Other animals have suction cups to stay put!

bluespotted stingray

sea urchin

anemone

clown fish

Many reef animals need one another to survive. Some offer safe places to live. Others share their food.

Some fish and shrimp are cleaners. They remove dead skin and **parasites** from larger animals!

yellow-edged
moray eel

Pacific
cleaner shrimp

The Great Barrier Reef

Location: **Coral Sea of the Pacific Ocean; off the coast of northeastern Australia**

Australia

N
W E
S

Great Barrier Reef

Size: 134,364 square miles (348,000 square kilometers); largest coral reef in the world

Water temperature: 75 °F to 85 °F (24 °C to 29 °C)

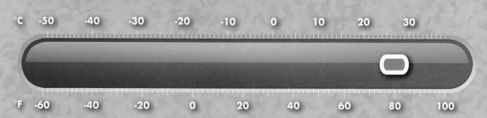

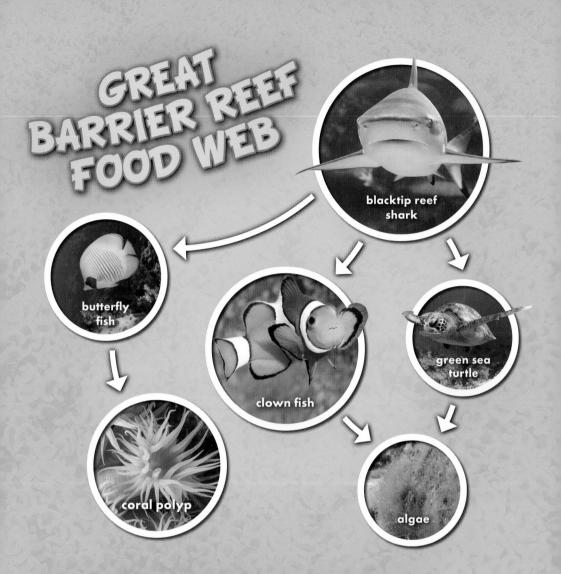

GREAT BARRIER REEF FOOD WEB

blacktip reef shark

butterfly fish

clown fish

green sea turtle

coral polyp

algae

Other important plants: red and green seaweeds, sea grasses, mangroves

Other important animals: sea anemones, jellyfish, octopuses, sponges, starfish, cuttlefish, crabs, giant clams, whale sharks, bottlenose dolphins

Glossary

algae—plants and plantlike living things; seaweeds and most other kinds of algae grow in water.

atolls—ring-shaped coral reefs

barrier—a wall that blocks; barrier reefs separate shore from open ocean.

biomes—nature communities defined by their climate, land features, and living things

climate—the specific weather conditions for an area

coral polyps—the living ocean animals that build coral reefs

food chain—a system of who eats what in a biome

fringing—bordering; fringing reefs touch shore.

mangroves—tropical trees that grow in shallow salt water

parasites—living things that survive on or in other living things; parasites offer nothing for the food and protection they receive.

roots—the parts of a plant that keep it in place and take in water

skeletons—the frames of living things

tropics—a hot region near the equator

To Learn More

AT THE LIBRARY

Peterson, Megan Cooley. *Coral Reefs*. North Mankato, Minn.: Capstone Press, 2014.

Pfeffer, Wendy. *Life in a Coral Reef*. New York, N.Y.: Collins, 2009.

Rustad, Martha E. H. *Clown Fish and Sea Anemones Work Together*. Mankato, Minn.: Capstone Press, 2011.

ON THE WEB

Learning more about coral reefs is as easy as 1, 2, 3.

1. Go to www.factsurfer.com.

2. Enter "coral reefs" into the search box.

3. Click the "Surf" button and you will see a list of related web sites.

With factsurfer.com, finding more information is just a click away.

Index

animal adaptations, 12,
    16, 17, 18, 19
animals, 4, 5, 12, 14,
    16, 17, 18, 19
atolls, 7
barrier reefs, 7
climate, 6, 8, 9, 10, 11,
    12
coral polyps, 5, 12
food chain, 11
fringing reefs, 7
gases, 12
islands, 7
location, 6, 7
mud, 10
parasites, 19
plant adaptations, 12,
    13, 15
plants, 4, 11, 12, 13,
    14, 15
precipitation, 10
rain, 10
rocks, 10
roots, 15

skeletons, 5
sun, 8, 11, 13
temperatures, 9
tropics, 6
types, 6, 7
water, 8, 9, 10, 13, 15
wind, 10

The images in this book are reproduced through the courtesy of: idreamphoto, front cover (turtle); Ethan Daniels, front cover (background); strmko, p. 4; aquapix, p. 5; Tanya Puntti, p. 7 (top); Pete Niesen, p. 7 (center); R McIntyre, p. 7 (bottom); Borisoff, p. 8; David Doubilet/ Getty Images, p. 9; Micheal E. Long/ Getty Images, p. 10 (top); Mark Tipple/ Getty Images, p. 10 (bottom); Suzanne Long/ Alamy, p. 11; Stuart Westmorland/ Science Faction/ Corbis, p. 12; Antonio Martin, p. 13; Rich Carey, pp. 14, 16, 18; Vilainecrevette, p. 15; LauraD, pp. 17 (top), 21 (algae); almondd, p. 17 (bottom); James A Dawson, p. 19; JC Photo, p. 20; Ian Scott, p. 21 (blacktip reef shark); frantisekhojdysz, p. 21 (butterfly fish); Kletr, p. 21 (clownfish); Longjourneys, p. 21 (green sea turtle); Peter Leahy, p. 21 (coral polyps).